Can I Have Your Autograph?

The Hidden Secrets of Getting Autographs from
the Rich and Famous

Written by Brian Franco Harrin
Published By Comanche Press

Other books From Comanche Press:

The Islamic Conquest of Europe 2020

Helena, Texas: The Toughest Town on Earth

Guess Who's Listening at the Other End of Your Telephone?

A Manager's Guide to Guerrilla Warfare

FIRST EDITION
Copyright © 2013
By Brian Franco Harrin
Published in the United States of America
By Comanche Press
906 Lightstone Drive, San Antonio Texas 78258

Email: canihaveyourautograph1@gmail.com

Website: http://canihaveyourautograph.net/

ALL RIGHTS RESERVED
ISBN: 978-0-9626012-7-9
Library of Congress Catalog Control Number: 2013901029

This book is dedicated to all the autograph collectors who take pride in preserving and cherishing the snapshots of history captured in the form of autographs.

I also want to thank my family for supporting me and all the great signers past and present.

Table of Contents

PREFACE

My intention in writing this book was to offer people a definitive resource on autograph collecting, to help them be aware of the various types of non-authentic signatures, and to inspire those who may not know much about the hobby to experience the sense of fulfillment many collectors enjoy with the ownership of signatures from all sorts of genres.

INTRODUCTION

If you think that autographs are just for kids, then you're in for a real shock. Over three million people now collect autographs in this business that generates more than $4 billion a year. If you somehow find an original William Shakespeare autograph at your local garage sale, you are now worth nearly $3 million!

Autographs are a snapshot of history captured in time, but many folks today wonder whether or not they have a "truly" authentic autograph, where they should purchase autographs, what are their autographs worth, and how do they get into the hobby?

If you are asking yourself any of these questions, I strongly urge you to turn the page and put your mind at ease with the wealth of insight presented in this book. I have been enjoying the hobby of autograph collecting since I got my first autograph from San Antonio NBA player Antonio Daniels at a basketball camp I participated in when I was a young kid. That moment sparked a lifelong interest in the hobby, and now I am going to share different areas of knowledge on the subject of collecting—from purchasing "real" autographs, to figuring out how to detect fake signatures, as well as how to collect autographs through the mail.

After you turn that first page, you will be well informed on all things associated with autograph collecting, and you will not be the unfortunate one who gets ripped off on fake autographs.

I stopped believing in Santa Claus when I was six. Mother took me to see him in a department store and he asked for my autograph.

— Shirley Temple

Figure 1: Shirley Temple from the 1933 short film *Glad Rags to Riches* (Public Domain)

Chapter 1: The Beginnings of Autograph Collecting

As an autograph collector myself, I was always curious about how it all started. How did this whole hobby come about and what were the origins of its creation?

The earliest account of a form of autograph collecting begins in the 16th century with German students. The traveling scholars kept books containing letters of correspondence written by people that they had encountered during their "Wanderjahren" or journeys.

Their album collections served as a sort of filing system for letters of introduction for the student at future destinations along his travel or route. The value of these autographs was their ability to open doors for the students, rather than the value of the actual handwriting of the signers as we've come to known the hobby currently.

A form of autograph collecting that we could associate with today started in the later 18th century when people of leisure started to assemble collections of correspondence and various literary manuscripts written by the famed men of politics and letters. The main objective at the time was to collect monumental figures from the past, such as the famed poet John Milton.

As the 19th century rolled along, people began to expand their collections to living authors and statesman, whom they had admired. These early autograph collectors had some main justifications regarding collecting, one being for historical purposes—to preserve the documents or correspondence of an important figure—and the other being to showcase the collector's social prominence because although there wasn't a marketplace established for autographs, to have access to them meant you were a respected figure in the various social circles.

Now focusing on America, autograph collecting did not begin here at home until about 1815. Early accounts from the 19th century hail William Sprague of Albany and Israel Tefft of Savannah as the first big autograph collectors although they soon would be followed by many others.

These early American collectors were in a different position in relation to their European counterparts because of an unavailability of distinctive American literature, leaving the hungry autograph collectors to focus on the writings of respected national and local statesman. It was not until the influx of national literary figures such as Washington Irving and their contemporaries that autograph collecting in America shifted into full force.

An increased demand helped fuel the development and creation of a commercial marketplace for autographs. With the first generation of American autograph collectors silently disappearing, their collections began winding their way to the public via auctions, which were first held in England in the 1830s and later in America.

In 1850, the famous literary figure James Fenimore Cooper wrote a letter to autograph collector Mrs. Hamilton Fish saying that he would have no trouble sending her a dozen autographs as he received and complied with such requests from perfect strangers "almost daily." I guess Mr. Cooper got just a little bit of fan mail!

Political figures begin receiving autograph requests in the mail, and some folks even had the courage to ask for locks of hair! Don't try that today! During the 1848 presidential campaign, Zachary Taylor was receiving many such requests, something that his cousin James Madison would have never seen in his 1812 campaign. In 1860, Abraham Lincoln had so much fan mail coming in that he set secretaries to fulfill the requests for his signature—hence the beginnings of the dreaded "secretarial" signature.

Figure 2: James Fenimore Cooper, Circa 1850 (Public Domain)

New York City was booming in the 1880s, and a great sense of pride and excitement sparked around the city. A lot of new and old money was being spent on personal collecting. Establishments such as the American Art Association auction house sprung up like wildflowers as the collecting bubble expanded.

In 1887, Walter R. Benjamin opened the first likely shop selling autographs and manuscripts on Broadway. That next year, Francis Madigan founded a similar business, and both of these establishments enjoyed great public reception and success. Later on, some famed autograph dealers in Philadelphia and Boston had some interesting customers such as the business tycoon J.P. Morgan and even US President Franklin D. Roosevelt!

Figure 3: A street scene in New York City, taken on Broadway Street, Circa 1897 (Public Domain)

By middle of the 19th century, there were recreational clubs devoted specifically to autograph collecting, and by 1890 there had already been one popular periodical devoted solely to collecting autographs called *The Collector*, followed by full-length books on the growing subject.

Figure 4: A clip from the autograph periodical *The Collector*, Circa July 1890 (Source: http://mysentimentallibrary.blogspot.com/2011/09/my-autograph-letter-collection.html)

A big shift in the culture of the early 20th century reflected upon autograph collecting. While the main targets of the collectors were still literary, political, and high-ranking religious figures, motion picture, radio, and television stars began to come into the picture.

Many terms have been used to describe "passionate and competitive" autograph hunters, such as "autograph hound" and in the 19th century "autograph hunter," which was known as a derogatory term for the folks who were particularly aggressive in their approaches or who resorted to deceitful tactics to obtain signatures.

In 1939, Walt Disney tapped into the market, producing a cartoon called "The Autograph Hound," in which Donald Duck sneaks around a Hollywood studio lot in a quest for his favorite celebrities. Even a book, *The Autograph Hound,* was published in 1973 by John Lahr to shine light on these pesky autograph seekers.

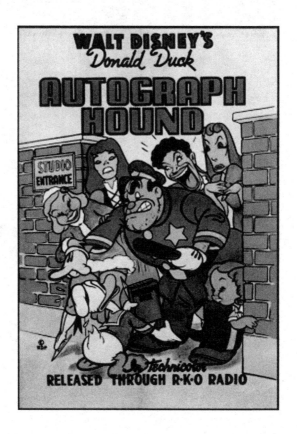

Figure 5: A theatrical poster from the 1939 cartoon "The Autograph Hound"

(Source: http://en.wikipedia.org/wiki/The_Autograph_Hound)

And as we fast-forward to the present, something called the Internet comes roaring into view. Autograph websites, chat rooms, and message boards are blessings for the modern autograph collector. Now, we can get our favorite star's address via online databases although some work better than others. Magazines and publications devoted to autograph collecting are readily available. And some website called "eBay" makes purchasing autographs a collector's reality.

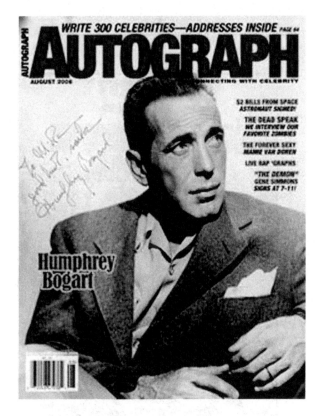

Figure 6: An autograph collecting magazine from 2008. (eBay)

Perhaps the most amazing and remarkable aspect of autograph collecting is its longevity. For a period of over two centuries, autograph enthusiasts have taken personal pride and fulfillment in obtaining the scribbles of selected individuals. Although I can't predict the future, I firmly believe autograph collecting will become even bigger, igniting the same spark that people for centuries have shared in perfect harmony.

CHAPTER 2: WHO TO COLLECT?

You are probably wondering to yourself, as I did, "Who should I collect?" As you learned in the previous chapter, in the past, autograph collecting was pretty darn specific to major literary and political figures in society. I wonder what some of those early autograph seekers would think when they see people trying to stampede each other and going crazy over a Lady Gaga autograph. They might be rolling over in their graves just thinking about it.

Figure 7: Lady Gaga signs autographs for fans in Asia. (Public Domain)

I am sure you have the general genres in mind like sports, history, movies, music, but there truly is a vast array of areas people would never even think to collect. Some big idols I had when I was younger and playing basketball all the time were David Robinson, Tim Duncan, Kobe Bryant, and so forth. As I began to really expand my parameters and learn more about history, I became even more intrigued with more elevated role-models such as Thomas Edison, Ronald Reagan, Harry Truman, Henry Ford, Ray Kroc, Abraham Lincoln, and countless others.

Figure 8:President Ronald Reagan, taken when he was involved with the General Electric Theatre. (Public Domain)

It really all comes down to who you personally admire, who inspires and intrigues you, who has influenced your life, and even who your favorite respective individuals are. Some people have favorite presidents that they would like to have autographs from, movie stars that they really enjoy, and singers whose music they listen to all the time.

I know in my personal collection of autographs, I am intrigued by all sorts of people. I have a variety of autographs in my collection: Jimmy Carter, George W. Bush, Newt Gingrich, Jane Fonda, Noam Chomsky, Kirk Douglas, Chris Matthews, Bill O'Reilly, Carl Lewis, Maya

Angelou, John F. Nash Jr., Huey Lewis, and so many more. But you get the idea.

Figure 9: Actress Jane Fonda doing a book signing in 2005.(Public Domain)

Some areas you may not have thought about include business (e.g., J. Paul Getty, finance) or the military (e.g., Medal of Honor heroes such as Pappy Boyington and famed generals such as Norman Schwarzkopf). There are autographs to collect from the realm of aviation, such as from Howard Hughes and Amelia Earhart, as well as the highly collected space genre, from astronauts such as Neil Armstrong and John Glenn. You might also consider exploration, science, medicine, inventors, and authors such as yours truly or Nobel Prize winners such as John Steinbeck.

Many people want autographs from the cast of their favorite movies and TV shows such as *Forest Gump* and *The Walking Dead*. There literally are so many fields you can collect, but the collection revolves around your desires.

Figure 10: WW2 hero Pappy Boyington (Public Domain)

Figure 11: Famed aviator Amelia Earhart (Public Domain)

Some advice I would give to a new collector of autographs is to try to think outside the realm of the well-known folks and include names that the average person may have never heard of but who have played a huge role in history. For instance, I bet most people have heard of and would know of Thomas Edison, the famed inventor of the phonograph, the motion picture camera, and something called a light bulb!

But have you ever heard of a guy named Nikola Tesla? I would bet money that most people have never even heard of the guy, and he is the man responsible for allowing you to charge your iPads and cell phones in your house. He is known for his contributions to the design of the alternating current electrical supply system, or AC. Get this—he even worked along with Thomas Edison before he ventured out on his own!

Figure 12: Nikola Tesla, Circa 1890 (Public Domain)

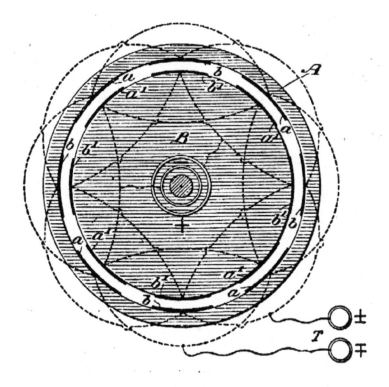

Figure 13: A depiction of a Alternate Current Electrostatic Induction Apparatus from Tesla, Circa 1891 (Public Domain)

My overall point is that you should collect autographs from people who significantly interest you, people whom you admire, who intrigue and inspire you, and with whom you have a connection, such as favorite movie and TV stars, music stars, historical figures, and sports icons.

Sometimes people collect autographs just for the monetary connection. Although this might make them a pretty penny, the human connection is the one area that the majority of collectors share. This hobby is one that brings to life history and captures a moment forever.

There are countless areas of collecting, and it's up to you now to venture off and step foot into the autograph-collecting world.

CHAPTER 3: BUYING AUTOGRAPHS

Wait! I know you're eager, but before you start taking out your checkbooks and credit cards—ready to buy autographs—I am going to go over the many factors associated with buying autographs.

Obviously, an easy and economical way for many collectors to buy their most wanted autographs would be through the Internet. In my view, one website stands out as the leading champion of available autographs, which is none other than eBay. eBay is an online marketplace that allows people to easily purchase and sell products and merchandise in one place. With the click of a button, you can have a multitude of autographs readily available in seconds.

Figure 14: eBay Corporate Headquarters in California. (Public Domain)

There are many categories you can look under, such as collectibles, books, sports memorabilia, etc. If you have a specific person's autograph in mind, you can simply enter them in the search box and see what comes up. For example, let's say I want a Wilt Chamberlain autograph; I would simply enter that exact phrase on eBay and take a gander at what comes in the results page.

You can even organize the search results according to price, time listings, best matches, most and least bids, etc. You can either use the "Buy it now" function, which basically means you agree to the seller's price and must pay the set amount listed, or you can try bidding for an item, hopefully getting the price you feel comfortable spending.

Now, just because someone lists an autograph on eBay as "authentic" or includes a "certificate of authenticity" at a low price, this does not necessarily mean it's real. As the old saying goes, if it's too good to be true, it probably is.

I would use extreme caution when purchasing autographs on eBay and do some research before making a purchase on the signer's signature, signing habits, etc. I personally would look for autographs that have been looked at by a respected third-party authenticator, such as PSA/DNA or JSA, and that have the appropriate COA. I will go more in depth on authentication in the next chapter.

Figure 15: A screenshot of eBay, searching "Wilt Chamberlain autograph" (Brian Harrin)

Autographs come written in many forms, such as on trading cards, cut signatures, checks, books, documents, memorabilia, magazines, etc. Some people prefer one type more than others, but all are collectible.

A good tip I would give you is if you are going to buy an autograph, aim for signed checks. You can bet that the actual person most likely signed their own check although I have seen cases where this was not the case. But in my view, this is a lot safer than, let's say, a signed scrap of paper or picture. I also tend to see signed checks sell a lot higher in eBay auctions, probably for this reason.

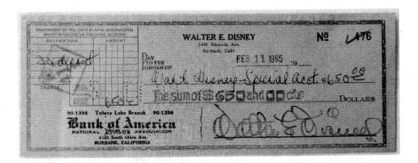

Figure 16: A Walt Disney authenticated, signed check (eBay)

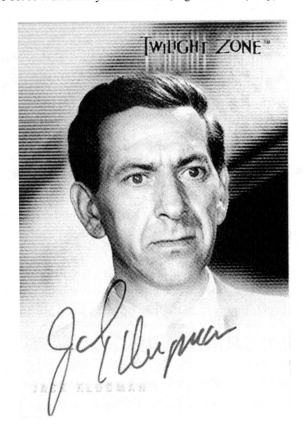

Figure 17: A Jack Klugman signed, authenticated trading card from the TV show *The Twilight Zone* (eBay)

Figure 18: A Neil Armstrong authenticated, signed cut (eBay)

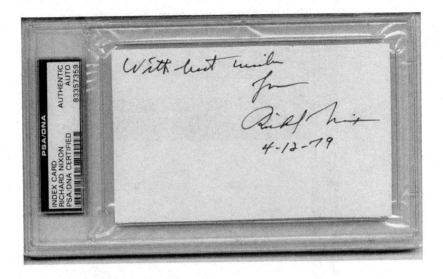

Figure 19: A President Richard Nixon authenticated, signed index card (eBay)

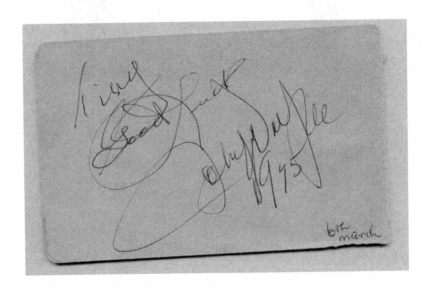

Figure 20: A John Wayne authenticated, signed album page (eBay)

Figure 21: A Muhammad Ali authenticated, signed boxing glove (eBay)

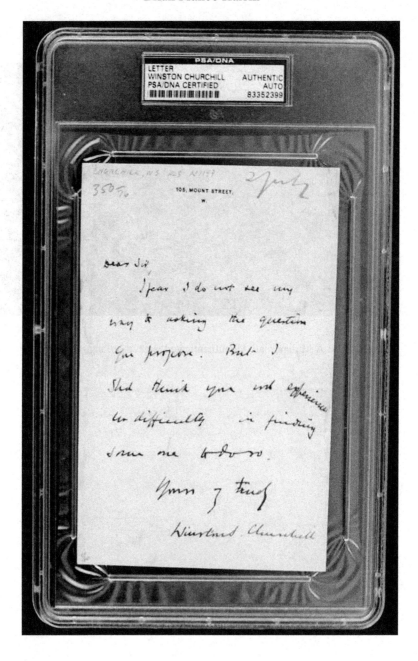

Figure 22: A Winston Churchill authenticated, letter signed (eBay)

Figure 23: A Mickey Mantle authenticated, signed baseball (eBay)

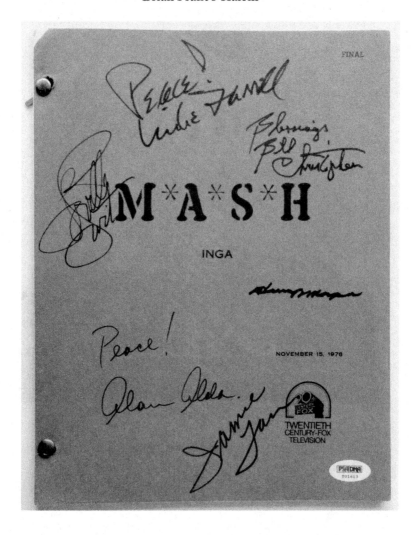

Figure 24: A authenticated cast signed script from the TV show *MASH* (eBay)

Figure 25: A Tiger Woods authenticated, signed golf cap (eBay)

Figure 26: A Stan Musial authenticated, signed magazine (eBay)

Figure 27 : A Joe Paterno authenticated, signed photo (eBay)

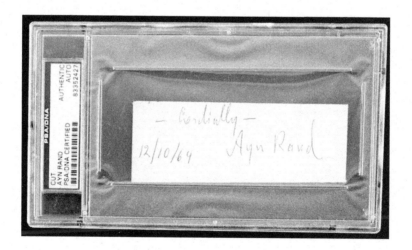

Figure 28: A Ayn Rand authenticated, signed cut (eBay)

Figure 29: A B.B. King authenticated, signed guitar (eBay)

Figure 30: A Angelina Jolie authenticated, signed photo (eBay)

Figure 31: A Fidel Castro authenticated, signed photo (eBay)

Figure 32: A Ozzy Osbourne signed, authenticated trading card (eBay)

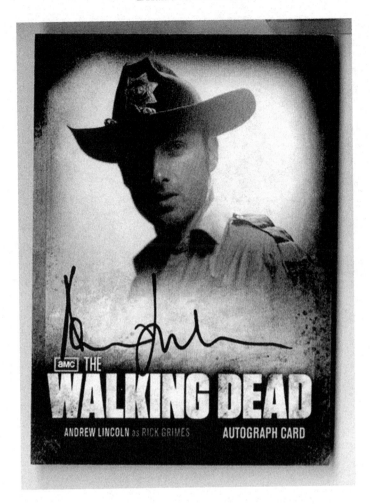

Figure 33: A Andrew Lincoln signed, authenticated trading card from the TV show *The Walking Dead* (eBay)

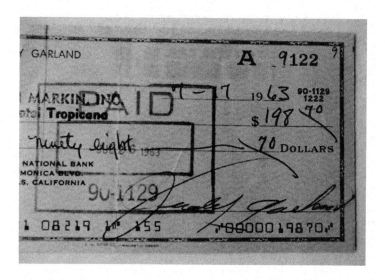

Figure 34: A Judy Garland authenticated, signed check (eBay)

Figure 35: A Jackie Robinson authenticated, signed index card (eBay)

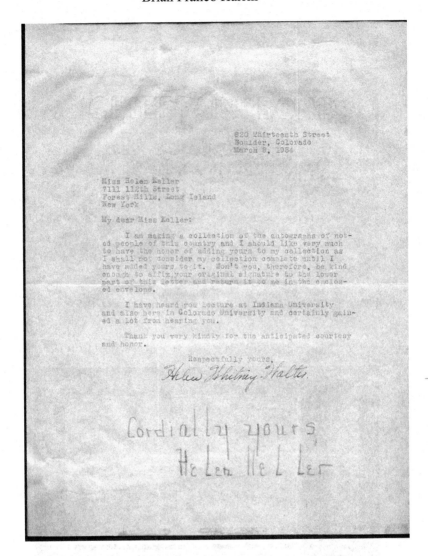

820 Thirteenth Street
Boulder, Colorado
March 8, 1934

Miss Helen Keller
7111 112th Street
Forest Hills, Long Island
New York

My dear Miss Keller:

I am making a collection of the autographs of noted people of this country and I should like very much to have the honor of adding yours to my collection as I shall not consider my collection complete until I have added yours to it. Won't you, therefore, be kind enough to affix your original signature to the lower part of this letter and return it to me in the enclosed envelope.

I have heard you lecture at Indiana University and also here in Colorado University and certainly gained a lot from hearing you.

Thank you very kindly for the anticipated courtesy and honor.

Respectfully yours,

Helen Whitney Walter.

Cordially yours
Helen Keller

Figure 36: A Helen Keller authenticated, signed letter (eBay)

Figure 37: A Clint Eastwood authenticated, signed photo (eBay)

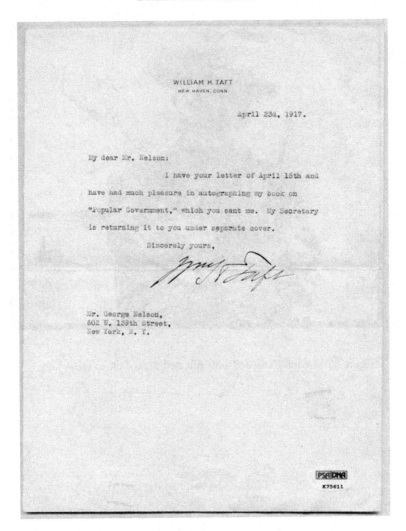

Figure 38: A President William H. Taft authenticated, typed and signed letter (eBay)

Figure 39: A President George Washington authenticated, signed cut (eBay)

Figure 40: A Charles M. Schulz (Creator of Peanuts comic strip)

authenticated, signed sketch (eBay)

Another bit of my two cents I would give to you is to look at an organization called the Universal Autograph Collector's Club or UACC, which was founded in 1965 and is the hobby's largest organization in the world.

They offer collectors memberships for about $35 a year, which include an award-winning magazine sent to you filled with articles and news in the autograph-collecting world, information on upcoming educational events and conventions, and updates on the latest forgeries, rubber-stamped signatures, autopens, and more. As a member myself, I feel it's a great buy and resource to utilize.

When buying from autograph dealers, it is very beneficial for you to see if they are UACC registered dealers. Note, I said registered—not members. While a seller might say they are a UACC member, this does not necessarily mean they are offering authentic items; they simply pay their dues for the membership as I do.

If, on the other hand, they are registered dealers, they are vetted and monitored by the UACC to ensure they are doing business in an honorable fashion. For these folks to be registered dealers with the UACC, they must provide the UACC references and experience, as well as pertinent information regarding their business.

Another good organization that many autograph dealers are linked with is the Professional Autograph Dealers Association or PADA. This organization caters to dealers specifically and is another great credential to look for when shopping with autograph dealers, whether they are on eBay or their respective individual websites.

A very popular venue for buying autographs is autograph conventions. Although I personally have not been to such a convention, they are a great way to meet your favorite stars in person and get an autograph that you know is actually 100 percent authentic because you saw it signed right before your very eyes. One such convention is called the Hollywood Show, and it has conventions in Los Angeles, Chicago, and Las Vegas. They have tons of signers, and you can even get your photo taken with the celebrity, depending on each person's policies.

Figure 41: Autograph collectors at a 2006 "Doctor Who" convention (Public Domain)

The next time you get your local newspaper or cruise on over to craigslist.com, check out the garage sale and estate sale sections. These can be great opportunities for people to get autographs at very reasonable and sometimes bargain prices. Be aware that some sellers may play you as a fool and tell you some story about how they got it signed in person or know its 100 percent real. My only advice is to use common sense and look to see if it's an obvious fake, whether it is pre-printed, autopen, etc.

If you happen to find an autographed item that looks good, look it up on your smartphone via eBay, and check for a PSA/DNA or JSA example to see if matches or looks very similar. If it does and if the price isn't that high, I would take the gamble and see if you struck it big! Then you can get it authenticated later and enjoy it for years to come!

I personally only buy autographs that I can afford; if it sounds too high, they are probably trying to get as much out of you as they can. Overall, these could be golden and sometimes rare opportunities for an autograph collector's dreams to come true!

Some other great places to get autographs are thrift stores, such as Goodwill and The Salvation Army. Scan through the book section and check the inside covers to see if they are autographed. Usually, if they are personalized, they are most likely authentic. I have seen examples of people finding books signed by Cal Ripken Jr. or Jimmy Carter at dollar prices. You really never know what you can find, and these are great ways to get inexpensive autographs, or autographs on a budget! Just use common sense and caution, as with all autograph buying.

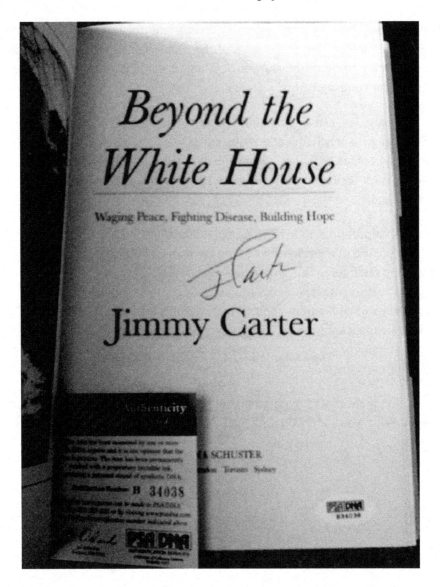

Figure 42: A President Jimmy Carter authenticated, signed book (eBay)

Also, if you have a Half Price Books store or another used book store down the street from you, it is probably worth the trip. Look at the signed-book section, or ask one of the employees where they keep them. Then you can see if you can score any big hits such as a Buzz Aldrin signed book or maybe even a Mickey Mantle signature. Sometimes, Half

Price Books has specials going on or coupons for holidays, and those come in handy to lower the costs of these books. You never know what people may bring in the store to sell, and it could end up being a huge name that you may be lucky enough to eventually own.

Lastly, you can score great in-person autographs at book signings. Some huge names frequently write books, whether they are autobiographies or fiction, and this may be the ultimate opportunity for you to meet them in person and get a 100 percent-authentic signature in your hand.

A helpful tip is to save your book-signing ticket and maybe take a quick picture of the celebrity signing the book, just in case you wanted to sell it in the future. This will help tremendously with a higher selling price, because you have proof of the signing, in part acting as your certificate of authenticity. Some great websites for checking upcoming book signings are www.celebritybooksigningsandevents.com and www.findbooksignings.com/ where you can be up to date on future book signings in a town near you.

So go ahead and mark your calendars for the next book signing that appeals to you, and you can start building your autograph collection today!

Figure 43: Newt Gingrich signs books for the public in 2012. (Public Domain)

Figure 44: Famed boxer Mickey Ward has a book signing in 2012. (Public Domain)

By now, you should have a good idea of the approach you want to take regarding purchasing autographs. Each of these ways has its own advantages and disadvantages, but remember, the only way to know 100 percent that your autograph is authentic is to see it signed right in front of your very eyes!

CHAPTER 4: IS IT REAL OR NOT?

Okay, Mr. Author, get to the meat of the bone. How can I tell if an autograph is authentic? I am sure this is the common thought shared by my readers, so hopefully I will tackle some of the questions you might have.

Autographs are something generations of collectors have enjoyed and passed on to their loved ones. Unfortunately, non-authentic or fake autographs have ended up in family collections, dealers' inventories, on eBay, and through the mail.

In fact, did you know that in the early 1990s, the FBI launched "Operation Bullpen," which was a harsh crackdown on memorabilia forgeries centered in the hot market area of Chicago, where you had Michael Jordan and other local athletes' signatures being faked daily? Pretty crazy stuff right?

Figure 45: A Michael Jordan authenticated, signed check (eBay)

As I previously mentioned, the only way you know 100 percent that you have an absolutely real autograph is to see the item signed in person. That's it! But soon you will know terms such as "autopens," "stamped," "secretarial," "ghost-signed," and "pre-printed," and you will be able to spot them with ease.

Whether, you are buying autographs or got one in the mail, you have to look at many factors. First, we are looking at pre-prints or pre-printed signatures. Basically, pre-prints are born with a celebrity signing a photo, and then that exact same photo becomes mass produced with the signature already on it.

Pre-printed autographs are actually part of the photo, and in effect, non-authentic. Luckily, these types of non-authentic signatures are pretty easy to spot on your own.

So let's say you have a signed photo, and you want to see if it's pre-printed. I would first hold the photo up near your eye level at an angle, toward a good source of light, and look at the signature. If you see the signature under the gloss or if it disappears entirely, you have a strong indication that the signature is pre-printed.

With a hand-written signature, it will appear on the "top" of the gloss and will not disappear when you hold it at an angle toward the light. A helpful tip is that if you get a signed picture in the mail from Studio Fan Mail, it is always going to be a pre-print or autopen. Also, take a look at the ink itself—a Sharpie will have a distinct look to it, as will a pen.

Next, I would look up the celebrity's signature on the Internet and see if you see the exact same signed photo. And by exact, I mean the ink, signature, placement, etc. are all spot on. If you see multiple examples of this, you know you have a pre-print.

The last suggestion would be a LAST resort if you really have doubts about the signature: Find a small corner of the autograph and dab a tiny amount of alcohol or nail polish remover onto it with a Q-tip. If the Q-tip removes that section of the autograph, it obviously wasn't preprinted, and you might have just ruined your signed photo! Ouch!

You can also wet your finger and rub it across a portion of the signature and see what happens. If it smears, you had a hand-written signature. I would caution you to use these methods as a last resort and not risk damaging the signature. Now you can finally decipher a pre-printed photo from hand-signed ones!

Figure 46: A *Storage Wars* pre-printed signed photo (Brian Harrin)

Second, have you ever heard of a stamped signature? It's exactly what you are thinking, a rubber-stamped autograph. These are probably the easiest to detect. I personally have seen my share of stamped signatures from people I had written through the mail.

Some things to look for would be uneven ink distribution, where the ink tends to pool at certain points, and often you see sections where there is no ink at all! The signature will often bleed or be smudged on the item. The rubber-stamped signature will not share the natural slant or flow of a hand-signed autograph. This is due to the rubber stamp being simply placed straight down onto the item, so no pen strokes are present.

Lastly, you will see a rectangular "haze" around the autograph, where the edge of the rubber stamp touches the item. Although these types of signatures are easy to spot, always keep a good eye out for them because they are out there!

Figure 47: A Jerry Lee Lewis stamped autograph—notice that only his signature is stamped. (Brian Harrin)

Imagine for a second, you are a well-known celebrity, and you are getting hundreds—maybe thousands—of autograph requests a month.

Do you think for a moment that if you were really busy or had many obligations, you could sign for each and every individual? No way. What would you do? Well, you might say, "I will just have a family member or secretary sign for me," and hence our next topic, the secretarial signature.

Secretarial signatures or items that are "ghost signed" have been around for hundreds of years. Many documents supposedly signed by kings of France up through at least Louis XVI were actually signed by their secretaries.

As you learned in the first chapter, Abraham Lincoln was getting so many autograph requests in the mail that he had a secretary sign for him personally. Throughout history, US presidents, dating back to George Washington, have employed secretaries to handle their correspondence for them. Early on, most of these presidential secretaries did not attempt to imitate the president's handwriting, but rather acted as a proxy signer.

This changed, however, in the 20th century when the secretarial signatures become very similar to the real thing. They have tricked autograph collectors for years. Once the secretary learned to sign, they would inevitably sign the exact same way each time. So in effect, if there is dissimilarity between the secretary and the genuine signature, the secretarial signature will show that distinction every time.

Figure 48: A photograph of President Harry Truman, with his secretary: Rose Conway in the Oval Office, Circa 1947 (Public Domain)

Some US presidents utilized more secretaries than others, but perhaps no other president employed as many secretaries as John F.

Kennedy did, who literally had dozens of secretaries skilled at forging his signature. So if I were you, I would probably be extra cautious the next time you are shopping for a JFK signature.

Secretarial signatures got a lot tougher to spot starting with President Lyndon B. Johnson, but fortunately some notables planted a "key" to distinguish authentic from non-authentic, such as LBJ putting a dot under the letter "B" when he signed, or Jefferson Davis's wife adding a period after the name when she signed for her husband. These things are good to know right? Another good tip is if the celebrity is a male, look to see if the signature is feminine looking as this would be a good sign of a secretarial, assuming he had a female secretary of course.

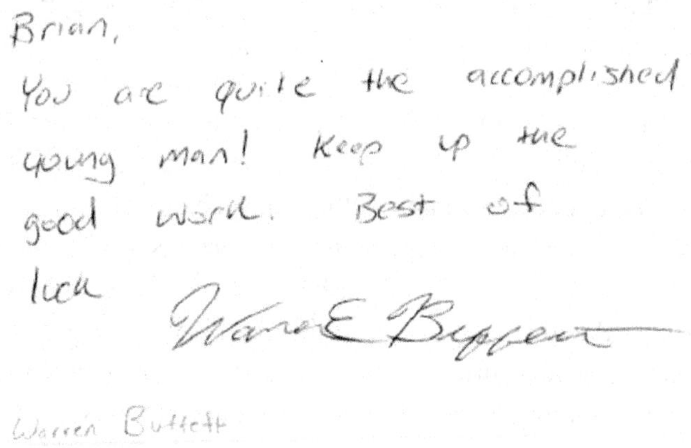

Brian,

You are quite the accomplished young man! Keep up the good work. Best of luck

Warren E Buffett

Warren Buffett

Figure 49: A Warren Buffett secretarial autograph, checked out by a professional graphologist (Brian Harrin)

Figure 50: A Warren Buffett authenticated, signed picture—see the difference? (eBay)

Movie and TV stars have actively sent out secretarial signatures from past to present. In the past, some known secretarial signers through the mail were Frank Sinatra, Bob Hope, Ronald Reagan (whose mom was his signer), Marlon Brando, John Wayne, Charlton Heston, Katherine Hepburn, and many more.

Today, some you see are Robin Williams, Al Pacino, John Travolta, Robert De Niro, Clint Eastwood, Morgan Freeman, Carrie Fisher, and many more.

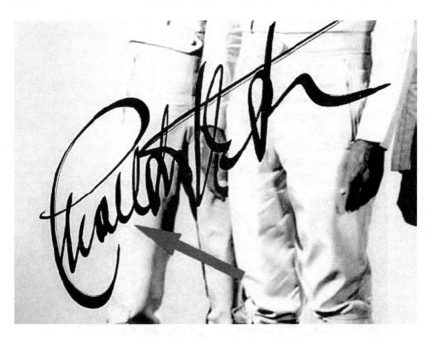

Figure 51: A Charlton Heston secretarial signature, obtained through the mail—notice how the "r" looks like a lower cased "L."

(Source: http://zipper68.blogspot.com/2011/03/your-charlton-heston-autograph-its.html)

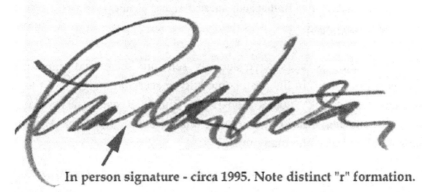

In person signature - circa 1995. Note distinct "r" formation.

Figure 52: A Charlton Heston authentic signature obtained in person—notice the difference with the "r."

(Source: http://zipper68.blogspot.com/2011/03/your-charlton-heston-autograph-its.html)

It all boils down to research, research, and research! Look at the celebrities' in-person autographs if available; look at PSA or JSA certified examples; read about their signing habits and their uses of secretaries; and use common sense. Educating yourself is the best thing you can do to be aware of autograph fakes and is my #1 advice on this subject!

How many of you have ever heard of something called an autopen? Unless you really know about autographs, I would bet not many of you have. And that is perfectly okay because you will finally know what it is, and when asked by Alex Trebek on Jeopardy, you will win big!

The autopen has actually been around longer than you might think. No later than 1804, Thomas Jefferson started to use a polygraph machine (like an early autopen), that copied out letters as he wrote them, and he kept these copies for his own records.

Figure 53: A modern reproduction of a polygraph machine similar to the type President Thomas Jefferson used, Circa 1974. (Public Domain)

The autopen is basically a machine that utilizes a real pen and real ink to draw an exact replica of an autograph. The owner makes templates with different examples of his signature. His secretary then inserts one of the templates into the machine, which is used to sign correspondence. The secretary can use this magical machine to sign correspondence at rates of hundreds per hour!

Autopens have been in general use since the 1940s and are used mainly by presidents, public officials, astronauts, and others who have too much mail to respond to. President Eisenhower began resorting to autopens in the late 1940s, and he actually took them with him to the White House. President Kennedy started using an autopen at the beginning of his presidential campaign in 1959 and used it until his death, although as you remember, he probably preferred having one of his dozen secretaries sign.

Presidents from Johnson forward have used autopens to sign everything from regular, routine letters to really important documents. I even read about a story recently where President Obama used an autopen to sign the Patriot Act extension into law!

Luckily, there are some ways to detect the pesky autopen. Look for a shaky signature, which would indicate the movement of the machine in operation. Try to spot light signatures, especially ones that do not have a variation in pressure as seen by an indentation in the paper when viewed in light.

If you see abrupt pen stops or a "drawn" look to the signature, that is a good tell. I personally have received many autopen signatures in the mail, and I always look for shakiness and ink dots at the start and end of letters.

Some autopens, especially in the earlier years, left little deposits of extra ink at the beginnings and ends of names or the breaks, where the machine had stopped in its track. Also, numerous autopen patterns are more legible than the actual signer's signature, so if you find an example where you can read clearly every letter in the signature that is usually more of a scribble, you probably have an autopen.

Some of the newer autopens now include a standard or impersonal greeting in addition to the signature to help it look more realistic (e.g., "Best Wishes" and then a signature). Thankfully, none prior to about 2007 inscribed an item to a specific individual or wrote any individualized content.

So when looking to buy autographs, try to look for ones that are inscribed to an individual or have inscriptions because chances are those are not autopens.

Figure 54: A Mitt Romney autopenned signed photo—notice the shakiness and dots at the beginnings and ends of letters because of the autopen machine stopping. (Brian Harrin)

Figure 55: The infamous autopen machine, hard at work!

(Source: http://www.tampabay.com/news/article1177511.ece)

Nowadays, a whole lot more people use autopens, from sports stars, to famed movie and TV figures, politicians, and many notable people. Just be on the lookout for them and keep up to date with known autopen patterns, which you can do by joining organizations like the UACC.

Believe me, it took me a while to see the difference between an autopenned signature and a real one, but you will soon be able to spot them with ease!

Lastly, I want to talk to ya'll about authenticating autographs you have or ones you want to buy. I personally recommend using either PSA/DNA or JSA.

Like you've heard me say a lot now, seeing something signed in person is the only true 100 percent guaranteed authentication service. Authentication is a tricky subject and many folks have varying opinions on the topic.

One of these companies is called Professional Sports Authenticator or PSA, and they claim to be the largest and most trusted third-party grading and authentication company in the world. According to their website, "they are the preferred choice of collectors, dealers, and auction houses worldwide and have processed over 20 million cards and collectibles, having a declared value of over a billion dollars." That's a lot of business! They also mention on their website that "in 1998, because of the influx of widespread counterfeiting, forgery, and piracy, they formed PSA/DNA, which is the world's leading third-party authentication service." They claim to have evaluated over three million autographs since 1998, and have been analyzing astonishing amounts each year.

The other authenticator I trust would be James Spence Authentication or JSA. Their methods of analyzing autographs are similar to PSA/DNA, and they are well respected in the business.

Now, I am not going to tell you that they are 100 percent perfect in authenticating autographs because they are not. I have seen mistakes made by them and many others, but no authenticator is perfect 100 percent of the time. I personally trust them the most compared to any other authenticator because of their background, the leading experts they have, and the process they use to authenticate autographs.

So overall, my personal preferences are PSA/DNA or JSA, when I look to buy an autograph or send one I received for them to authenticate. Whatever you do, please research the signer's autograph and look at their signing examples, especially ones they did in person, so you can be well informed, just like the experts!

Hopefully now you have a better understanding of the many types of non-authentic autographs out there and how to safely buy and have signatures authenticated. Authentication is a touchy subject for many of us, and we can all learn from each other's experience and expertise in the field!

CHAPTER 5: WHAT ARE AUTOGRAPHS WORTH?

Autograph collecting is not only a great hobby but it can also be worth a whole lot of money too. As you read in my introduction, if you happen to stumble upon a William Shakespeare autograph, guess what? Your net worth just went up $3 million!

When there are three million autograph collectors worldwide and a business making $4 billion a year, this isn't just another hobby.

There are many determining factors when breaking down how much autographs are worth, and we will review many of the big bullet points. First to consider is how well known was the person (if deceased), or if they are currently alive, how prominent are they now? If you got an autograph from an actor whom no one has really heard of compared with somebody like Humphrey Bogart, which one would have more value? Of course it's Bogart because people remember him and his movies. It all comes down to notoriety and social prominence, as these are two driving factors behind an autograph's value.

Figure 56: A screenshot of Humphrey Bogart, from the film *The African Queen*, Circa 1951 (Public Domain)

Second, you look at the scarcity of the autograph. Remember supply and demand from economics class? Well, that's the lesson here.

For instance, the famed actor Jimmy Stewart was a very accommodating and generous signer; therefore his signature won't be as worth as much compared with somebody like actor James Dean, who died suddenly at the age of 24. You'd be right to guess that there are not many of Dean's signatures out there. Even right now, there are quite a few Barack Obama signatures out there, but the demand is high because of his rising notoriety. So remember, see how scarce someone's signature is, and this will give you a good barometer on their autograph value.

Figure 57: A Jimmy Stewart authenticated, signed index card (eBay)

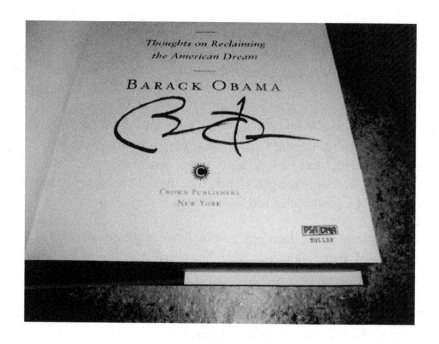

Figure 58: A President Barack Obama authenticated, signed book (eBay)

Figure 59: A James Dean authenticated, signed check (eBay)

Third, what type of item is signed? For example, ask yourself, would you rather have a signed 8" x 10" of Harrison Ford from *Star Wars* or his signature on a blank index card? Easy decision, right? Well, that's my case in point.

Typically, the least valuable items are small pieces of paper, from autograph albums to index cards or a cut signature. Next you have documents, which can be legal agreements, contracts, even checks. This is followed by a typed, signed letter; then signed photographs; and last but not least, a handwritten and signed letter.

The nature of the document and content can greatly affect its value. For example, Babe Ruth's signature on a check is worth $5,000 or more, but if you had a signed contract of his to play ball for the New York Yankees, you would be looking at a value many times that amount! There are many other items that can be worth lots of money, but the key is to consider what kind of item is signed.

Figure 60: A Harrison Ford authenticated, signed photo from *Star Wars* (eBay)

Fourth, you have to look at the condition of the autograph. People do not want to buy autographs that are barely readable or have coffee stains all over them. It isn't happening. They want a nice, crisp-looking signature that is presentable. Condition is so crucial in autograph collecting and can affect the value of a signature in a heartbeat.

Rips, folds, creases, damage, etc., can drastically change the value of an autograph. So, if you have autographs or if you purchased ones, do your part to keep them in pristine condition and away from dangerous elements. Then when it comes to selling your items, you can get the most profit. Remember, you are in part, whether you know it or not, curators of history, and it's up to you to preserve the past so that generations ahead can enjoy them just as you did.

Figure 61: A barely visible Babe Ruth authenticated, signed cut (eBay)

Lastly, you want to see how long the person lived—as morbid as it might sound—and how approachable or unobtainable they were with autographs. Typically, after a person dies, their autograph goes up in value. Why? Well, because they aren't around to sign any more autographs, therefore diminishing the supply.

If you have someone who lived a long time, they probably signed a whole bunch compared with someone like the famous country singer Hank Williams who died at the age of 29. So remember that when considering value. You also need to look at how approachable somebody is (or was) for autographs. For instance, Greta Garbo was not too fond of signing autographs, while President Jimmy Carter is a very willing and gracious signer.

Figure 62: Actress Greta Garbo, Circa 1939 (Public Domain)

Also, social trends affect an autograph's value: When the movie *J. Edgar* came out, his autograph went up in value. Events like this reconnect people with a person, therefore creating more buzz and interest and increasing the demand and value for an autograph.

Figure 63: The famed Hank Williams, who died suddenly at the age of 29 (Public Domain)

Figure 64: A movie poster for *J. Edgar* (eBay)

To give you an idea as to what some autographs go for, according to PSA/DNA in 2012, here are some current values:

Sports autographs:

- Babe Ruth: a signed cut, $3,000; a choice, single-signed baseball, $60,000 or more

- Lou Gehrig: a signed cut, $3,500; a choice, single-signed baseball, $75,000 or more

- Michael Jordan: a signed cut, $175; a signed basketball, $600 or more

- Muhammad Ali: a signed cut, $150; a single-signed boxing glove; $500 or more

- Tiger Woods: a signed cut, $250; a single-signed golf flag, $1,500 or more.

Not too bad right?

How about some historical and entertainment autographs:

- Elvis Presley: a signed cut, $1,500; a signed contract or letter, $35,000 or more

- Neil Armstrong: a signed cut $1,500; a signed photo, $5,000 or more

- John F. Kennedy: a signed cut $1,750; a presidential letter or document, $25,000 or more

- Marilyn Monroe: a signed cut $2,500; a signed photo, $15,000 or more

- Walt Disney: a signed cut $750; a signed photo, $3,500 or more

These examples should give you a good indication that autographs can be worth money—a lot of money!

You now have learned that autographs can be quite valuable and all the determining factors associated with their value. It's important to remember these factors when purchasing and obtaining autographs from the past and present, and I wish you great success!

Chapter 6:
Obtaining Autographs Through The Mail

Are you looking for a less expensive and easier way to obtain autographs from your favorite celebrities? You have come to the right place my friend because I know the secret: collecting autographs through the mail, or (TTM) for short.

I stumbled across autograph collecting through the mail in April of 2012. I was searching for more information about it on the web after it piqued my interest, and I decided to give it a try for myself. I had read some general guidelines and advice, but as I experienced TTM collecting firsthand, I developed my own personal method of success and will share some of that with you.

Currently, I have over 250 authentic autographs that I have gotten in the mail, and all it cost me was postage and some supplies. That's it. So what do you say we dive into the topic?

As you probably remember from Chapter 1, collecting autographs through the mail is not a brand-new phenomenon. Remember how James Fenimore Cooper received autograph requests "almost daily," and this was in 1850! So, it's been around for a little while.

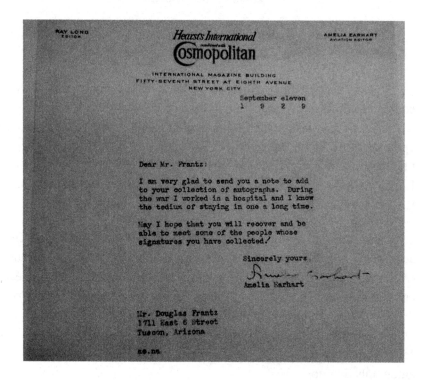

Figure 65: An Amelia Earhart authenticated, typed and signed letter, notice how she is responding to an autograph request. (eBay)

It really picked up steam with rising social trends and celebrities popping up like popcorn. And with autograph magazines providing celebrity addresses or databases of addresses available with the click of a button, people now collect TTM worldwide.

So let's say you decide you want to try this TTM thing and see if it works for you, but you're not sure what it is. Basically, you find an address for a celebrity; write him or her a polite letter asking them for their autograph; send an item to be signed; enclose a self-addressed, stamped envelope (or SASE); and partake in something called the waiting game. If your letter is received well, you just might get back an autograph. And that is TTM in a nutshell.

Before we even go any further, though, I am going to give you some helpful advice. Believe me—you will thank me for this.

I want you to open Microsoft Excel or the equivalent on your computer and create your own database of celebrities you want to send letters to. (If you need help with operating Excel or the equivalent, look up some tutorials on the Internet; YouTube is a good source.) I would title the first column "**date sent**" and list each entry according to the date I mail the letter, for instance "1/3/2013." This way you can see what is still out there and how long it took to come back in your hands.

Title the next column "**celebrity name**," and list each entry according to name and what their famous for, like "Jason Alexander (Actor/*Seinfeld*)." Title the next column "**date received**," and list each entry as you receive it with the date of receipt, for example, "February 2, 2013." The next column should be titled simply "**autographed?**" Yes, with a question mark because sometimes you get your stuff back with no John Hancock on it. So, you would enter "yes" or "no" if it's autographed or not.

The last column should be titled "**real or fake**," and here is where your detective work comes in handy. If you received an autograph, check to see if it's in line with other in-person autographs or authenticated ones. If so, then you would enter "real." If it's obviously a fake, whether it's an autopen, secretarial, preprint, stamped, etc., enter that in the box.

This way you can have a good count of the number of authentic autographs in your collection. And that's the way the cookie crumbles. This will help you so much if you decide to do TTM and will keep you very organized.

Next, you need the most current address for the celebrity you want to write to. If you are on a budget, a good free resource that I used personally for a while is called Fanmail.biz, which is at http://www.fanmail.biz/. There you can find helpful information, some decent addresses, and a good forum to communicate with other autograph collectors. As mentioned, this is a free website.

I later discovered one website called Star Tiger, which is the best website out there for this hobby, in my view. Yes, good things sometimes come at a cost, but at $4.99 a month and access to over 370,000 addresses, I'd say it's one heck of a deal. You can find it at http://www.startiger.com and I highly recommend this site if you are serious about TTM collecting. It is updated daily, with hundreds of changes per day. You can see what other people received and compare that with what you receive. Probably the coolest feature for me is to see in-person signed autographs of a celebrity that people post in the gallery. Then you can compare that with what you receive.

You can do so many more things with this site and communicate with folks who have been doing this for a long time. It is worth every penny, and I urge you to try the "free tour" on the site to see if you like it. I would say I have gotten over 90 percent of all my autographs from this site.

Another cool tip is after you find a good address resource you like, try something called Via Venue or (VV). Do you ever hear on the radio that someone like Brad Paisley or Maroon 5 will be in town at such and such date and time?

Well, Via Venue refers to writing to a celebrity at a venue where they are playing or performing and sending it so that it gets to them in time for their performance date. For example, let's say I want to send to Brad Paisley VV. I would send him my letter, the item to be signed, an SASE, and I would address it to the place he is performing, sending it so that it gets there in time for his performance. If I'm lucky, the venue will pass it on to Mr. Paisley, and when he has a break, hopefully he will sign my item and send it back to me.

Figure 66: Country musician Brad Paisley performing at a concert in 2007

(Public Domain)

Are you going to be 100 percent successful? Nope, but it definitely is worth a try, and I have had great luck doing this. It also works very well with stars performing in Broadway plays. Check out http://www.playbill.com to see the current and upcoming plays, along with addresses, etc.

YouR Name
Address
City, State
Zip code

VV
EXAMPLE

Please hold
for XYZ
on 3/1/13.

XYZ Singer
XYZ venue
Address
city, State
Zip Code

Do NOT
Bend

Figure 67: An example of how to address a Via Venue envelope (Brian Harrin)

Next up, you need to have some supplies ready to start doing TTM, which depend on what you want to send out to celebrities for them to sign. I personally send only 3" x 5" blank index cards, and yet I have received many signed photos, etc. Just keep your requests to one to two items because remember they are doing you a favor by signing.

Don't be greedy or they may end up not signing at all! You can send 8" x 10" pictures, 5" x 7", 4" x 6", whatever you want. Just remember, whatever you send, you might not get it back. So if I were you, I would not send your rare baseball cards or expensive merchandise—don't send something you cannot afford to lose. Also, remember that shipping heavier items will cost more in postage. Be aware that some celebrities are signing only their books, so those are always a good item to send.

Figure 68: Playing cards are another popular item to send TTM (Public Domain)

But to give you an idea of supplies to get, I use regular blank computer paper for my letters, blank 3" x 5" index cards for signing, strip and seal envelopes that are 4 1/8" x 9 ½" for shipping and for the SASE. And that's it. All these items are inexpensive. It just depends on your budget and what you want to get signed, which is entirely up to you. You can find more information on materials, etc., on the TTM sites.

Now for a huge part of the process—the request letter. I prefer to handwrite my letters because I feel it shows that you took the time to write to them personally, and they will appreciate that.

I know some prefer to type letters, but I highly recommend handwriting. This is typically referred to by a celebrity as "fan mail," and you can only imagine how many letters some of the bigger celebrities get a week. So if I were you, I would keep your letters down to a page, max. Writing 10 pages might not work so well!

Most of these folks do not have time to read three pages about how you liked them in their movies. (I mean, how would you feel if you had to personally read pages and pages of fan mail?) First, I would date the letter at the top and then address it to the person appropriately, like "Dear Mr. Ford." Then I would separate my letter into three paragraphs, the first telling who I am and my successes and goals/ambitions.

To me, this is key. You should emphasize your accomplishments like "I just got a trophy in basketball," or "I graduated from Harvard University." But be honest! You get the point, though. You need to stand out from the crowd.

The second paragraph is about the celebrity. This is where you praise them and talk about why you admire them, etc. I would research what movies, etc. they were in and mention this in the paragraph. Also, try to talk about something that they are not necessarily known for, like if you wrote to Tim Duncan, talk about your admiration for his charitable work or his off-the-court activities. This might just pique their interest.

In the last paragraph, you politely ask for an autograph. You would say that you know they are really busy, but you would appreciate it if they signed your item. This is key: Thank the person for taking the time to read your letter. They will appreciate that. Then, you can write "Sincerely" or "Best wishes" and sign.

But don't use that handy autopen at your desk to sign—try to sign them yourself! Just kidding, but if you want their autograph, it's only appropriate for you to sign too. And that's it. You will eventually have your own style, but this should steer you in the right direction.

Quickly, I will go over what the self-addressed, stamped envelope (SASE) is. It's an envelope on which you write your name and address in the "from" area (upper left corner) as well as in the "destination" area. It's from yourself, to yourself. Simple, right?

Then put postage on it, and you're ready to go. Typically, for things like index cards or trading cards, you need just one stamp on the outgoing envelope and the SASE. But for heavier, larger items, you will need more postage. Sending an SASE with your TTM is so crucial because all the celebrity has to do is put your autographed item in your SASE and seal it, and it's ready for them to drop in the mailbox. They don't have to worry about postage or anything. Doing this will greatly increase your chances for a response and is a common courtesy. Also, I would write "Do Not Bend" in bold letters on both the outgoing envelope and the SASE so that the post office knows to handle with care. Do they always listen? No, but it's safer to do it than not have anything on there.

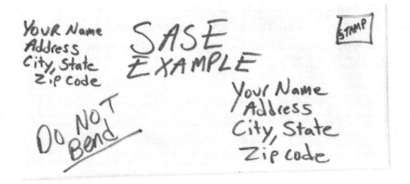

Figure 69: An example of how to address an SASE (Brian Harrin)

The last area I will touch upon is storage and how you can take care of the things you receive. If sending index cards, I would recommend storing them in pocket pages that are archival quality and acid free, and I would put them in a good-size binder. You should also store letters, notes, etc. in acid-free sheet protectors. You can find many supplies on Amazon, and I highly recommend them.

For photos, etc., I would suggest using photo albums or framing them, using archival quality and acid-free materials. Just make sure you keep your items in a safe place, away from sunlight, and that you use good storage items to keep them in. You can find more information on storage tips via the message boards on the TTM websites.

Finally, after all that hard work, you play the waiting game. Responses will come in days, weeks, months, and yes, even years. Also, you may never hear back from a celebrity or get your package returned to you. This is part of the hobby. Patience is your friend.

Figure 70: A welcoming sight for any TTM collector! (Public Domain)

I would say the majority of my responses have been in the time range of one to three months. It all depends on the celebrity. Also, I wanted to tell you to be realistic when considering whom you perceive will respond TTM. I know you want a Harrison Ford and an Angelina Jolie autograph, but chances are the big stars do not mix well with the TTM crowd. Those are tougher people to get, but nothing is impossible if you can find the right address.

If you can write to people out of the spotlight or people just beginning their careers, you will have better luck. You will see some of my successes from TTM in the upcoming chapter on my collection.

TTM collecting is really the autograph collector's secret formula for obtaining a good number of autographs, without costing them an arm and a leg. Yes, you will get fake stuff back, but guess what? There are fakes up for sale also. If you educate yourself and are up to date with the hobby, you will stay ahead of the game.

CHAPTER 7: IN-PERSON AUTOGRAPHS

Imagine for a second you are a few feet away from Tom Hanks, making small talk with him as he signs your Forrest Gump photo. This can be a reality, with in-person autographs.

Sure, if you live in Small Town, USA, Tom Hanks is not likely to step foot into your local Piggly Wiggly, but if you happen to be on vacation in, let's say New York City, you never know whom you might run into!

Figure 71: Actor Tom Hanks speaking to a group of veterans in 2010 (Public Domain)

Figure 72: A Piggly Wiggly in Louisiana—don't see Tom Hanks yet, do you?

(Public Domain)

Want to know another reason that in-person autographs are ideal for the collector? You know for a fact that your autograph is 100 percent real, remember? It's a win-win situation as you get to meet your favorite celebrity and see them scribble right before your eyes.

Although I don't personally partake in getting in-person autographs very often, I bet I am missing out big time! A lot of major celebrities will sign for you in person, but remember, you might not be the only person trying to get an autograph. In fact, many people who get autographs in person do so for one big reason: They are not putting these autographs in their scrapbooks, if you get my drift.

These folks are professionals, and they bring lots of supplies with them. The one goal they have in mind is money, money, money. After they get items signed, they go right to websites (think eBay) to sell them, and that's how they might end up in your collection in the end. Now, that's their right and if that's what they do, so be it. There are many folks out there who genuinely want an autograph of a celebrity for their personal collection, rather than to sell it.

This is the modern reality of in-person autograph collecting, and I will give you some helpful tips if you decide to join in on the fun.

First, where would you find a celebrity in person? Well, usually in big towns like New York, Los Angeles, etc., but there are movie sets all over the place, performances at venues near you, and many other places. It requires research to find out where celebrities will be visiting, and you can do that by looking up their tour dates or visitations on the web or in newspapers. Then you will have a better idea as to where to look out for them.

Figure 73: Actor Aaron Eckhart signs autographs for fans at a European premiere of *The Dark Knight* (Public Domain)

I know some common places are outside TV studios, hotels, theatres, etc. If you happen to enjoy politics, as I do myself, then why not attend a political rally? Can you imagine if you got Obama's signature before he became president? These can be great places to meet your future public officials and get their signatures at the same time. It's all up to you to do the research and maybe you will get rewarded.

Figure 74: Actor Robin Williams signs autographs aboard the USS Enterprise (Public Domain)

Figure 75: President Gerald Ford at a campaign stop in Gulfport, Mississippi, Circa 1976 (Public Domain)

Figure 76: Vice President Joe Biden signs autographs by flashlight. (Public Domain)

Figure 77: First Lady Michelle Obama signs autographs for eager collectors in a comfortable setting. (Public Domain)

Second, I would arrive at the venue two to three hours early, depending on the venue. This will benefit you by allowing you a good spot to ask for autographs. Don't be the dummy who forgot to bring something to get signed—bring an item for the celebrity to scribble on: a picture, an index card, a CD, etc.

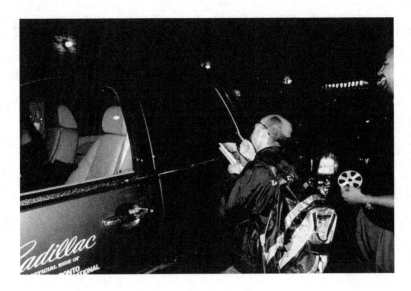

Figure 78: A last chance autograph opportunity, for a collector (Public Domain)

Also, don't be greedy. Limit your request to one or two items. Bring a good Sharpie for them to sign—one that works! Can you imagine a dry Sharpie ruining your autograph? That would be a nightmare. Blue sharpies seem to be a preference for collectors.

You might also want to bring a camera to take pictures of the celebrity (or with them if you're lucky) and remember that moment for years to come!

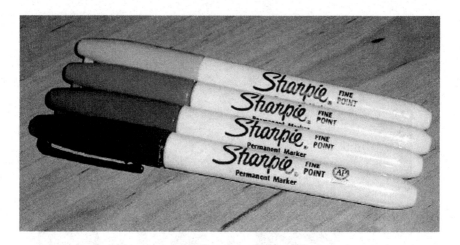

Figure 79: Don't forget your working Sharpies! (Public Domain)

Third, remember to be very respectful and courteous. Don't shout for autographs. Just use good etiquette and you'll be fine. Obviously, know a little something about the celebrity. Can you imagine this conversation: "Hi, Mr. Cranston, I am a huge fan!" He replies, "Oh yeah, what show did you like me in the most?" You reply, "Uhhh, all of them." Don't let this be you—know what they were in!

Figure 80: Actor Bryan Cranston signs autographs for knowledgeable autograph collectors. (Public Domain)

Lastly, try not to be too nervous when the celebrity is about to sign for you. This means no huffing and puffing, no sweat pouring down your face like a waterfall. Just be polite and ask them for an autograph.

They may accept your request or say they have to go, but it's all worth it if you get lucky and they sign. And please remember to thank the celebrity with a sincere thank you if they sign for you. You will remember these moments for a long time to come, and you will be glad you can tell everyone, you met so and so in person!

Figure 81: Don't let this be you when awaiting autographs! (Public Domain)

In-person autographs can be a rewarding and monumental experience for many people. If this sounds like something you want to try, go for it! You just never know who you might meet!

CHAPTER 8: THE ART OF SIGNATURE ANALYSIS

Now, you might be thinking, what is he talking about? Signature analysis? What is it and how does that relate to collecting autographs?

Well, let me ask you something. Did you know you can tell a lot about a person simply from their handwriting and signatures? Sure, you might see obvious things: If the signature is huge, you might say they like writing big, but there is so much more to signature analysis, and it just might pique your interest.

Handwriting analysis or graphology is an ancient science that has been around since the days of Aristotle. You see it mainly used in police work in forgery cases, but it really spreads across many areas.

So how does this stuff work? Well, handwriting is linked with the brain, and not the hand you write in. You have nerve impulses traveling down the arm into the hand, which then direct the fingers to maneuver the pen. When the ink hits the paper, it reveals the complex inner workings of the writer's body, mind, and spirit. Pretty cool, right?

The primary basis of handwriting analysis as a science is that every person in the world has a unique way of writing. Starting at a young age, we have style characteristics that become the underlying method of our handwriting.

Over time we developed individual characteristics that are completely unique to us and distinguish our handwriting from everybody else's. I mean, many of us don't write like we did in the first grade. Hopefully not! And although many people might share similar individual characteristics, the chances of those folks sharing 20 or 30 individual characteristics is so unlikely that many handwriting analysts would say it's impossible.

Some things handwriting analysts look for in your handwriting can be the upper loops, the lower loops, the size of the writing, the pressure, the slants, if the writing is angular or rounded, where the t's are crossed, where the i's are dotted, the margins, and so many other things—pretty interesting stuff.

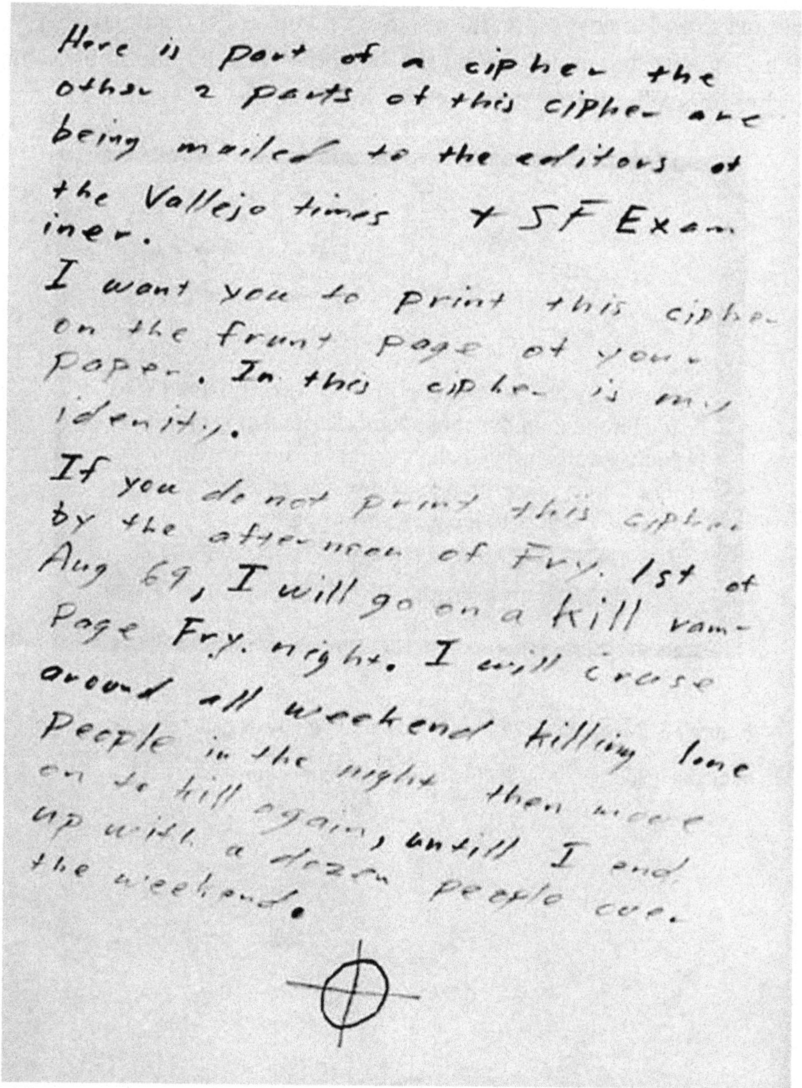

Here is part of a cipher the
other 2 parts of this cipher are
being mailed to the editors of
the Vallejo times + SF Exam-
iner.
I want you to print this cipher
on the frunt page of your
paper. In this cipher is my
identity.
If you do not print this cipher
by the afternoon of Fry. 1st of
Aug 69, I will go on a kill ram-
Page Fry. night. I will cruse
around all weekend killing lone
people in the night then move
on to kill again, untill I end
up with a dozen people over
the weekend.

Figure 82: The handwriting of the infamous "Zodiac" killer, Circa 1969 (Public Domain)

Handwriting analysis can tell quite a lot about a person. It's a reflection of our mood changes, which happen to be evident on the scribble you just wrote. You can find out a person's character and personality, physical health, mental health, energy, social development, sharpness, and many more things. So as you collect autographs, you might be able tell a lot about the celebrity just by looking at their handwriting. Who knew, right?

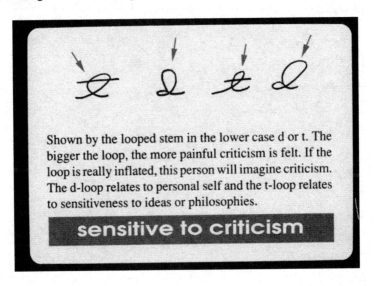

Figure 83: An example of how handwriting analysis can tell you a lot about someone (Source: http://handwritingnewsletters.com)

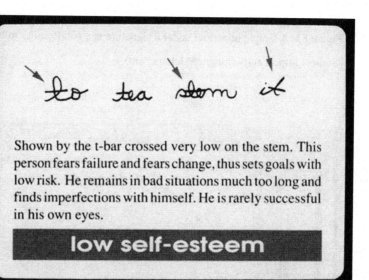

Shown by the t-bar crossed very low on the stem. This person fears failure and fears change, thus sets goals with low risk. He remains in bad situations much too long and finds imperfections with himself. He is rarely successful in his own eyes.

low self-esteem

Figure 84: How to detect low self-esteem from handwriting (Source:

http://handwritingnewsletters.com)

Revealed by an underline below one's signature. This person possesses strong leadership qualities, relies on himself, and has a great amount of inner strength.

self-reliance / leadership

Figure 85: A simple underline under a signature is a good quality to look for.

(Source: http://handwritingnewsletters.com)

Figure 86: An example of the underline signature trait, from actor Jack Lemmon (Brian Harrin)

This topic is so diverse. (If this subject piques your interest in the slightest, make sure to read the last chapter of this book.) So the next time you get that autograph on eBay or in your mailbox, take a gander at their handwriting and see what you can pick up. You never know what you might be able to see.

CHAPTER 9: MY PERSONAL COLLECTION

In this chapter, I am going to talk a little about my personal autograph collection, hopefully giving you some more ideas on who to collect.

Let's see, I have a William Shakespeare, George Washington, Abraham Lincoln, Marilyn Monroe—I wish. Maybe someday I will, but unfortunately not at this moment in time. I will split this up into ones I purchased and ones I got through the mail.

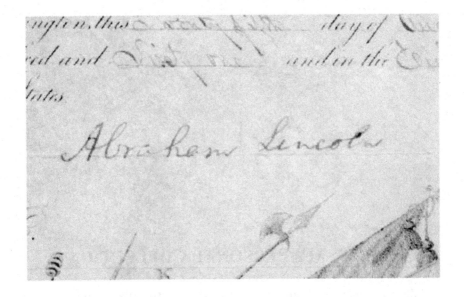

Figure 87: President Abraham Lincoln's authenticated signature, not in my collection, unfortunately (eBay)

So, as you remember, I trust PSA/DNA and JSA the most when it comes to buying autographs, and my collection includes a lot of signatures authenticated by them: a Joe DiMaggio signed first-day cover, a Jack Dempsey signed postcard, a David Robinson signed basketball card, a Dana Carvey signed index card, a Ray Bradbury signed index card, an Isaac Asimov signed index card, a George H.W. Bush signed cut, and a Calvin Coolidge signed cut.

Figure 88: Joe DiMaggio authenticated, signed first-day cover, my personal collection (Brian Harrin)

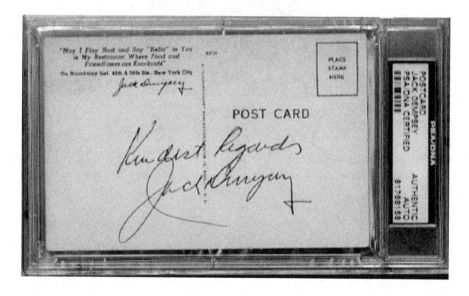

Figure 89: Jack Dempsey authenticated, signed postcard, my personal collection (Brian Harrin)

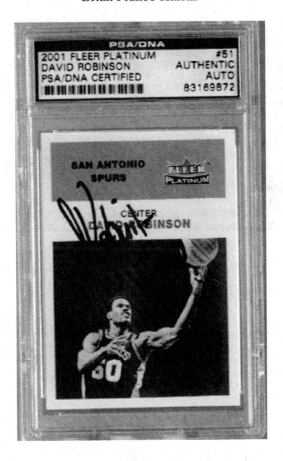

Figure 90: David Robinson authenticated, signed trading card, my personal collection (Brian Harrin)

Figure 91: Ray Bradbury authenticated, signed index card, my personal collection (Brian Harrin)

Figure 92: President Calvin Coolidge authenticated, signed cut, my personal collection (Brian Harrin)

I have several trading cards signed by basketball players, baseball players, people from *The Twilight Zone,* and some movie folks such as Gary Sinise.

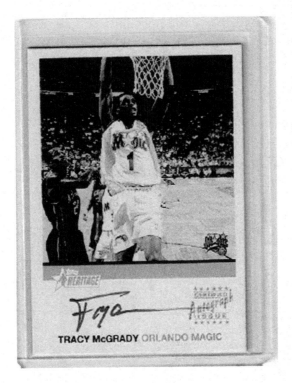

Figure 93: Tracy McGrady authenticated trading card, my personal collection

(Brian Harrin)

Some cut signatures I have are Pappy Boyington, Jack Haley, J. Edgar Hoover, Ray Liotta and Henry Hill dual cut, Jimmy Stewart, Richard Petty, Simon Lake, Ronnie Milsap, Pat Buchanan, Robin Roberts, and many others.

I have some signed photos from people such as Larry the Cable Guy, Robert McNamara, Brad Paisley, Jason Kidd, and so forth.

Now, TTM signatures. I personally collect signatures for my own collection and do not plan on selling any of them. Some that I have gotten through the mail are Jon Voight, Ed Asner, Dave Brubeck, George McGovern, and many military heroes, inventors, etc.

I also have Maya Angelou, Lauren Bacall, Dean Koontz, Jimmy Carter, George W. Bush, Tony Shalhoub, and folks from shows such as *Mad Men*, *The Twilight Zone*, *The Walking Dead*, and *Breaking Bad*. It's just a really diverse group of people in my collection. I also have gotten personal letters, etc. from many folks I had written TTM.

Figure 94: Comedian Phyllis Diller signed this photo to me TTM; she passed

away in 2012. (Brian Harrin)

Figure 95: Actor Martin Sheen signed this photo to me TTM. (Brian Harrin)

Figure 96: The famous "Jack" signed this photo TTM. (Brian Harrin)

Figure 97: President George W. Bush signed bookplate TTM (Brian Harrin)

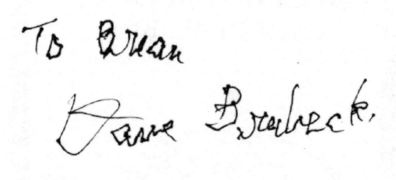

Figure 98: Dave Brubeck, a famous jazz pianist, signed this to me TTM; he

passed away in 2012. (Brian Harrin)

Figure 99: Carmen Basilio, a famous boxing champion, signed this to me

TTM; he passed away in 2012. (Brian Harrin)

Now that you have seen some of mine, it's time for you to get
started building your collection, or if you've been in the hobby for a
while, expand and collect many other interesting individuals. Then you

will officially become a curator of history and be in charge of saving the past so that all the future can see! Happy collecting!

CHAPTER 10: WHAT'S NEXT?

My hope is that after reading this book you are more informed and inspired by autograph collecting and that you decide to join in on the fulfillment many of us experience. You will be in good company, and share the same excitement as J.P. Morgan and Franklin D. Roosevelt had with autograph collecting.

Figure 100: Famed figure J.P Morgan, Circa 1903 (Public Domain)

Figure 101: President Franklin D. Roosevelt, a famed autograph collector

(Public Domain)

So what happens next? Well, in my next book, anybody whose interest was piqued by the subject of signature analysis will be greatly satisfied because that is the main subject of my next book.

I will go into greater depth discussing graphology, and hopefully I can guide you to become your own handwriting detective. You will also see a professional in the business analyze some famous people's handwriting, so stay tuned for that. It will be a wealth of information for anybody interested in the topic.

I also want to thank you for putting up with my sense of humor. I know you will be the first in line to buy tickets for my upcoming comedy tour.

All kidding aside, thank you for taking the time to read my book. I hope you gained an abundance of information and insight on the wonderful hobby we call autograph collecting!

ABOUT THE AUTHOR

Brian Harrin was born on October 24, 1992, in San Antonio Texas. He is a full-time college student, an Insurance agent licensed by the State of Texas, and is in the final stage of flight training for his Sport/Private Pilot license.

In addition to autograph collecting, Brian has performed multiple paranormal investigations of a South Texas ghost town working with TV documentary crews. He grew up participating in swimming, basketball, and the martial arts. Brian earned a First Degree Black Belt in Taekwondo at the age of 15 and is now training in the Israeli military self-defense system of Krav Maga.

RESOURCES

Shirley Temple Quote:

http://www.brainyquote.com/quotes/authors/s/shirley_temple.html

Introduction:

http://www.luxist.com/2008/01/29/the-world-of-rare-signatures-and-autographs-william-shakespeare/

Chapter 1:

http://www.rarebookschool.org/2005/exhibitions/autographs.shtml

http://www.raabcollection.com/blog/autograph-collecting-america-brief-history

Chapter 2:

http://www.padaweb.org/display_page.php?cid=7

http://www.schulsonautographs.com/shop/schulson/why-collect-autographs.html

Wikipedia: Edison, Tesla.

Chapter 3:

http://reviews.ebay.com/Autographs-Buying-Guide?ugid=394

http://uacc.org/

http://www.padaweb.org/index.php

Chapter 4:

http://www.sportsmemorabilia.com/articles-operation-bullpen

http://www.raabcollection.com/blog/authentication-check-paper-pen-and-ink

http://www.geocities.com/hollywood/set/7962/fake.htm

http://www.psacard.com/services/auto_authentication_process.chtml

http://www.hollywoodgoldenguy.com/Autographcollecting.html

http://www.astronautcentral.com/AutographBasics.html

http://reviews.ebay.com/Recognizing-STAMPED-autographs-from-AUTHENTIC-ones?ugid=10000000001240919

http://reviews.ebay.com/A-guideline-to-be-aware-of-autograph-forgeries-or?ugid=10000000001732595

http://www.geocities.com/~sbeck/secr.htm

http://www.raabcollection.com/blog/autograph-authentication-assess-evidence-secretaries-or-stamps

http://www.reocities.com/Hollywood/Cinema/3950/identifying_fakes.htm

http://www.raabcollection.com/blog/autograph-authentication-check-autopens-and-computer-generated-signatures

http://www.writeastar.com/forum/post/1916881

http://dailycaller.com/2011/05/27/obamas-autopen-signs-patriot-act-extension-before-midnight-deadline/

http://www.psacard.com/MostDangerousAutographs/2012/

http://www.politico.com/story/2013/01/autopen-barack-obama-10-facts-85720.html?hp=l1_b2

Chapter 5:

http://autographs.ha.com/c/ref/worth.zx

http://voices.yahoo.com/a-value-guide-autographs-signed-celebrity-photos-2792135.html

http://www.geocities.com/~sbeck/value.htm

http://www.psacard.com/guides/collecting_sports_autographs.chtml

http://www.psacard.com/MostDangerousAutographs/2012/

Chapter 6:

http://collectibles.about.com/od/entertainmentmusic/a/autographsmail.htm

http://www.wattographs.com/Resources/CollectingByMail.aspx

http://voices.yahoo.com/autograph-collecting-through-mail-2018497.html

http://reviews.ebay.com/Through-the-Mail-Autograph-Collecting-TTM?ugid=10000000002775521

http://www.freewebs.com/myautographcollection/collectingtips.htm

http://reviews.ebay.com/Secrets-For-Collecting-Celebrity-Autographs-By-Mail?ugid=10000000000797858

Chapter 7:

http://collectibles.about.com/od/entertainmentmusic/a/autographperson.htm

http://reviews.ebay.com/In-Person-AUTOGRAPHS-Collecting-Etiquette?ugid=10000000001759529

http://voices.yahoo.com/tips-collecting-sports-autographs-person-6501732.html

Chapter 8:

http://www.doctoroz.com/videos/what-your-handwriting-says-about-your-health

http://science.howstuffworks.com/handwriting-analysis.htm

CPSIA information can be obtained
at www.ICGtesting.com
Printed in the USA
FSOW04n1056231216
28791FS